On the Front Lines

The U.S. Navy SEALs at War

by Michael and Gladys Green

Consultant:
Mark Wertheimer
Historian and Curator
Naval Historical Center
Washington, D.C.

CAPSTONE
HIGH-INTEREST
BOOKS

an imprint of Capstone Press
Mankato, Minnesota

Capstone High-Interest Books are published by Capstone Press
151 Good Counsel Drive, P.O. Box 669, Mankato, Minnesota 56002
http://www.capstone-press.com

Library of Congress Cataloging-in-Publication Data
Green, Michael, 1952–
   The U.S. Navy SEALs at war / by Michael and Gladys Green.
      p. cm.—(On the front lines)
Summary: Provides an overview of the U.S. Navy SEALs, their mission,
members, history, recent conflicts, and modern equipment.
Includes bibliographical references and index.
   ISBN 0-7368-2159-7 (hardcover)
   1. United States. Navy. SEALs—Juvenile literature. 2. United States.
Navy—Commando troops—Juvenile literature. [1. United States. Navy.
SEALs. 2. United States. Navy—Commando troops.] I. Green, Gladys,
1954– II. Title. III. Series.
   VG87.G74 2004
   359.9'84—dc21   2002155629

Editorial Credits
James Anderson, editor; Steve Christensen, series designer; Jason Knudson, book
   designer; Enoch Peterson, illustrator; Jo Miller, photo researcher; Karen
   Risch, product planning editor.

Photo Credits
Defense Visual Information Center, 4, 7, 8, 15, 16, 19, 20, 23, 24, 26, 28
Photri-Microstock, 10
U.S. Navy Photo, cover

1 2 3 4 5 6 08 07 06 05 04 03

Table of Contents

CHAPTER 1

Learn about:

- SEALs in Afghanistan

- Organization

- Missions

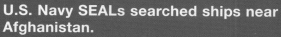

U.S. Navy SEALs searched ships near Afghanistan.

The U.S. Navy SEALs

After terrorists attacked the United States on September 11, 2001, U.S. Navy SEALs were sent to the country of Afghanistan. This country was a base for the terrorists. SEALs patrolled the Arabian Sea near Afghanistan. They boarded ships and made sure no weapons were being brought into the country.

SEALs also tracked and captured members of the terrorist group that attacked the United States. They made the terrorists tell where their weapons were hidden.

Nearly 1 million pounds (450 metric tons) of weapons were found. Terrorists had hidden the weapons in caves in the mountains of Afghanistan. The SEALs destroyed the weapons. Many terrorists then surrendered.

Who Are the Navy SEALs?

The SEALs are a 2,200-man unit of U.S. Navy Special Forces. Most of the Navy's Special Forces serve on SEAL teams. SEAL stands for Sea, Air, and Land. SEALs reach their targets by traveling across seas and oceans, in the air, and on the land.

Each SEAL team is made up of six platoons of 16 men. Congress does not allow women to serve as SEALs. Within each platoon are two officers and 14 enlisted men. The officers go through the same training as enlisted men.

In training and combat, the SEAL platoons divide into two squads of eight men. An officer commands each squad. In water operations, SEALs swim in pairs.

About 20 non-SEAL Navy members, both men and women, support each SEAL team. They do paperwork, fix weapons, and operate radios. They also control the team's supplies.

SEAL Team Missions

The Navy SEALs have five main missions. These are Special Reconnaissance (SR), Direct Action (DA), Combating Terrorism (CBT), Foreign Internal Defense (FID), and Unconventional Warfare (UW) missions.

SEALs work in pairs during water missions.

Some missions take SEALs into dangerous situations.

During SR missions, SEAL teams are placed behind enemy lines. The teams report on enemy forces and movements. They must do this without being seen.

SEAL teams on DA missions also go behind enemy lines. They attack and destroy troops and equipment.

In CBT missions, SEAL teams gather information on the location of terrorist groups. If a terrorist group has kidnapped U.S. citizens, the SEALs rescue them.

On FID missions, SEAL teams travel to friendly foreign countries. They teach foreign soldiers how to defend their own countries.

SEAL teams train friendly guerrilla forces during UW missions. Guerrilla forces are small armies that often use unconventional ways of fighting against a country's government.

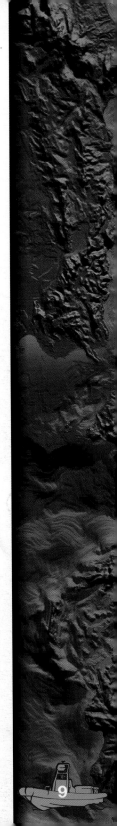

CHAPTER 2

Learn about:

SEALs approach a shore with weapons ready.

Italian Navy divers sank many ships in the early part of World War II (1939–1945). The divers used small underwater craft to move around. Other countries soon copied the Italians.

The Beginning

On November 20, 1943, U.S. Marines invaded a Japanese-controlled Island in the Pacific Ocean. As Marine boats approached the island, they ran into rocks under water. The Marines could not cross in the boats. They were forced to wade 700 yards (640 meters) to the island.

Japanese soldiers opened fire as the Marines waded through the water. The Marines had no cover. Hundreds of Marines died. Many were wounded and drowned in shallow water. The U.S. Navy decided it needed divers to check enemy beaches for obstacles.

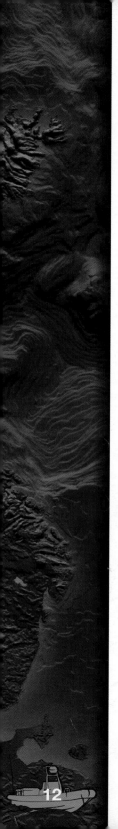

The first U.S. Navy dive teams were formed in 1943. They were called Combat Demolition Units. Their job was to sneak onto enemy beaches and blow up any obstacles that might get in the way of U.S. boats.

World War II

In 1944, the Combat Demolition Units were formed into larger groups. Their name was changed to Underwater Demolition Teams (UDTs).

By the end of World War II, the Navy had 34 UDTs in action. During a mission, the UDT men would check a beach landing site. They then would report what they found to their task force commander. If the commander gave orders, the UDT would return a couple of days later to destroy any obstacles.

Important Dates

1943—The first U.S. Navy dive teams are formed. These teams are called Combat Demolition Units.

1944—Combat Demolition Units are formed into larger groups. The new groups are called Underwater Demolition Teams (UDTs).

1950—Korean War begins.

1962—President John F. Kennedy orders the creation of Navy Special Forces teams. SEAL Team ONE and SEAL Team TWO are formed. The first SEAL teams arrive in South Vietnam.

1984—Remaining UDTs become SEAL teams.

1987—SEAL units are placed in the Persian Gulf.

1991—Operation Desert Storm begins.

2001—Terrorists attack New York and the Pentagon on September 11; SEALs are sent to Afghanistan.

2003—U.S. and Allied forces begin Operation Iraqi Freedom.

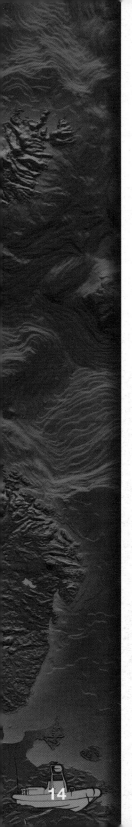

The Korean and Vietnam Wars

With the outbreak of the Korean War (1950–1953), the Navy's UDTs went into action. The UDTs now took on more dangerous missions. They blew up enemy bridges, radar sites, and railroad tunnels.

In January 1962, President John F. Kennedy decided the Navy needed a strong force. These experienced sailors would be dedicated to Special Forces (SF) missions. These missions would often take place behind enemy lines. SEAL Team ONE and SEAL Team TWO were formed.

The first SEAL teams arrived in South Vietnam in 1962. The North Vietnam army had attacked South Vietnam. SEAL teams trained the South Vietnamese. They taught them how to fight the enemy forces.

Beginning in 1969, the SEAL teams launched Direct Action missions. SEALs soon gained a reputation among the enemy troops. They were the most feared U.S. soldiers. The last SEAL team left Vietnam in 1972.

SEALs perform Special Forces missions.

CHAPTER 3

Learn about:

- Secret missions

- A fake invasion

- Fighting terrorism

16

SEALs conducted missions in the Persian Gul
during Operation Desert Storm.

Recent Conflicts

SEAL teams go wherever they are needed. Between the late 1980s and early 1990s, most operations were in the Middle East. To stop terrorism, SEAL teams have been to many locations that remain a military secret.

The Persian Gulf

Navy SEAL units were placed in the Persian Gulf from 1987 to 1989. The U.S. military called the events there Operation Earnest Will and Operation Prime Chance. SEALs protected civilian and military ships from Iranian naval attacks. Iran is a country in the Middle East.

The SEALs were based on two large barges in the middle of the Persian Gulf. From these locations, SEALs launched ship boarding, search and rescue, and surveillance missions.

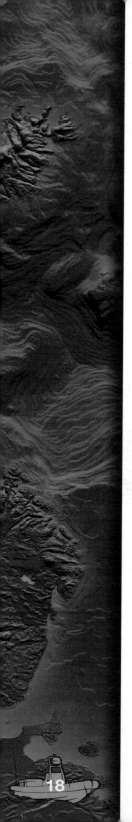

Fooling the Enemy

On January 17, 1991, U.S. and Allied forces launched a huge attack. The attack was aimed at Iraqi military targets. Iraq had invaded its neighboring country of Kuwait. U.S. leaders wanted to free the people of Kuwait from the Iraqi army. The mission was called Operation Desert Storm.

Before the Operation Desert Storm ground attack could begin, SEALs checked the Iraqi-controlled Kuwaiti coast. The SEALs looked for a site where troops could invade from the sea.

U.S. military officials decided not to invade from the sea. The SEALs were given a different mission. Their mission was to make it look like there would be an invasion.

The fake invasion took place during a nighttime mission on February 23, 1991. Navy SEALs placed explosives on a beach that Iraqi forces had claimed. The explosives were set with timers.

SEALs checked the coast of Kuwait during Operation Desert Storm.

The timers went off exactly when the U.S. ground forces began to invade from the opposite direction. The explosives made a loud noise. The Iraqi army thought that they were being invaded from the sea. More than 20,000 Iraqi troops raced away from the real land invasion. The Iraqi soldiers ran to fight the fake invasion.

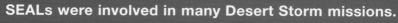

SEALs were involved in many Desert Storm missions.

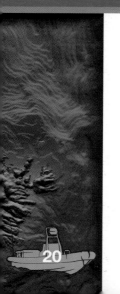

Other Desert Storm Missions

Navy SEALs also helped Kuwait capture an Iraqi-controlled island in the Persian Gulf. SEALs rode in Navy helicopters. They searched for Iraqi mines. Once the mines were spotted, the SEALs destroyed them with gunfire. Kuwaiti troops were then able to take over the island.

During any conflict, U.S. planes can be fired upon. On January 23, 1991, an Air Force F-16 fighter plane was shot down. The pilot had to eject from his plane into the Persian Gulf. Two SEALs in a Navy helicopter rescued him.

Operation Enduring Freedom

Terrorists attacked New York City and Washington, D.C., on September 11, 2001. Thousands of Americans and foreign visitors died because of the attacks. The home base for the terrorist group that planned the attacks was in Afghanistan.

A military group called the Taliban ruled Afghanistan. Taliban officials were asked to turn over the terrorists in their country. They refused. The U.S. government decided to stop more terrorist attacks by invading Afghanistan.

U.S. planes began to bomb Afghanistan on October 7, 2001. SEAL teams searched for terrorist troops and weapons. The last organized Taliban forces surrendered on December 6, 2001. SEALs continue to play an important role in fighting terrorism in Afghanistan and around the world.

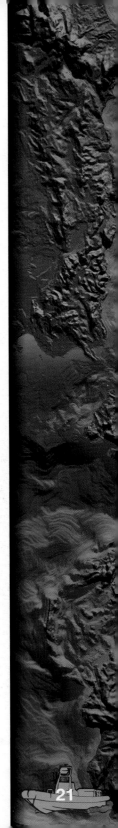

SEAL Training

SEALs go through some of the toughest training in the world. The course is called Basic Underwater Demolition/SEAL (BUD/S) training.

The BUD/S training course is divided into three separate parts. The first part lasts eight weeks. The fifth week of training is called "Hell Week." During this week, trainees are not allowed to sleep for five days. Trainees need to prove they are tough enough to survive in a war situation.

The second part of the BUD/S training lasts seven weeks. During this time, SEAL trainees learn to become underwater divers.

The final part of SEAL training lasts ten weeks. During this stage, the trainees learn to use weapons such as explosives.

If a SEAL trainee passes all three parts of the BUD/S, he continues. He then goes to a three-week Army parachuting course. After passing parachuting school, he is assigned to a SEAL team.

The trainee must continue to meet the high standards set by the SEALs. If he does, he will be awarded the gold trident, the badge of the Navy SEAL. He will become one of the U.S. forces' most highly skilled soldiers.

CHAPTER 4

Learn about:

- **Ground travel**

- **Underwater missions**

- **Future of the SEALs**

SEALs use DPVs to travel on land.

Today's SEALs

SEAL teams must be as close to trouble spots as possible. SEALs can respond on short notice to almost anywhere in the world. Once in the area, they have different ways of getting around.

Desert Patrol Vehicle

The Navy SEALs obtained a small number of dune buggies in the late 1980s. They call them the Desert Patrol Vehicles (DPVs).

DPVs travel well on sandy ground. Ships and planes carry them across the ocean to desert countries.

The three-man crew of a DPV sits in special bucket seats. They all wear seat belts. To talk to each other without shouting, they wear helmets with built-in intercom systems.

SEAL Team Arms

SEAL team members are armed with many weapons. These weapons include rifles and submachine guns. The standard rifle carried by a SEAL is the M4.

The M4 is a lighter and shorter copy of the M16A2 rifle used by Army and Marine soldiers. Like the M16A2, the M4 has a 30-round magazine. It can be fired on full automatic, or on semiautomatic mode.

The M4 was designed to have many extras that can be added or removed. They include a grenade launcher and a laser-pointing device. SEALs can also add a thermal imaging system. This system allows SEALs to see targets in the dark.

SEAL team members also carry the M60E3 machine gun (shown at left). The M60E3 was first issued in 1985. This weapon is lightweight and can be fired from a standing position, or while lying on the ground.

SEAL Team Boats

The newest boat used by the SEAL teams is called the Mark V Special Operations Craft (SOC-V). Its main job is to drop off or pick up SEAL Team swimmers. It often is used close to enemy shores. The SOC-V can be armed with four large machine guns.

An SDV can be stored inside a submarine.

The Patrol Coastal Ship (PC) is the largest boat used by SEALs. The PC is 170 feet (52 meters) long and 25 feet (8 meters) wide. It weighs 331 tons (300 metric tons). The PC is equipped with machine guns and cannons.

Mini Submarines

Another piece of equipment used by SEAL teams is the mini submarine. It is called the Swimmer Delivery Vehicle (SDV) Mark VIII. It can be carried and launched from a boat or larger submarine.

The SDV is stored inside the rear of a larger submarine. The speed and range of the SDV remain a military secret.

U.S. Navy SEALs Future

In March 2003, U.S. and Allied forces began Operation Iraqi Freedom. Some SEAL missions during this operation have not been released to the public.

Whether the SEALs arrive by sea, air, or land, they will be sent to defend the United States and other countries. Their training will continue to make the U.S. Navy SEALs some of the world's most feared soldiers.

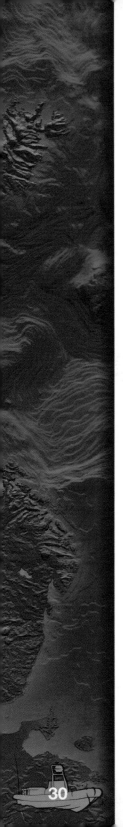

Words to Know

demolition (dem-uhl-ISH-uhn)—when something is destroyed

guerrilla (guh-RIL-uh)—a member of a small group of fighters or soldiers that often attacks a larger army

hostage (HOSS-tij)—a person who is being kept as a prisoner

reconnaissance (re-KAH-nuh-suhnss)—a military mission to gain information about an enemy

surveillance (suhr-VAY-lans)—to watch something closely; surveillance missions are launched to spy on enemy troops.

terrorist (TER-uh-rist)—someone who uses violence or threats to get what they want from a group of people or government; terrorists often act for political or religious reasons.

unconventional (uhn-kin-VEN-shun-uhl)—a way of fighting that is not like ordinary hand-to-hand combat; SEALs teach guerilla troops unconventional warfare.

To Learn More

Burgan, Michael. *U.S. Navy Special Forces: SEAL Teams.* Warfare and Weapons. Mankato, Minn.: Capstone Press, 2000.

Kennedy, Robert C. *Life with the Navy SEALs.* On Duty. New York: Children's Press, 2000.

Payment, Simmone. *Navy SEALs.* Inside Special Operations. New York: Rosen Publishing, 2003.

Useful Addresses

Naval Historical Center
Washington Navy Yard
805 Kidder Breese Street SE
Washington Navy Yard, DC 20374-5060

Naval Special Warfare Command
Public Affairs Officer
2000 Trident Way
San Diego, CA 92155-5599

UDT/SEAL Museum
North Hutchinson Island
3300 North A1A
Fort Pierce, FL 34949

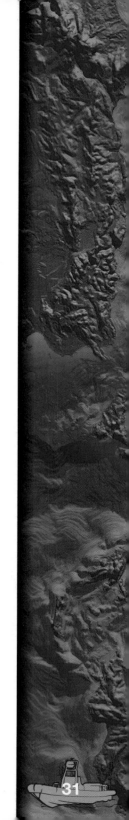

Internet Sites

Do you want to find out more about Navy SEALs?
Let FactHound, our fact-finding hound dog, do the research
for you.

Here's how:

1) Visit *http://www.facthound.com*
2) Type in the **Book ID** number: **0736821597**
3) Click on **FETCH IT**.

FactHound will fetch Internet sites picked by our editors
just for you!

Index

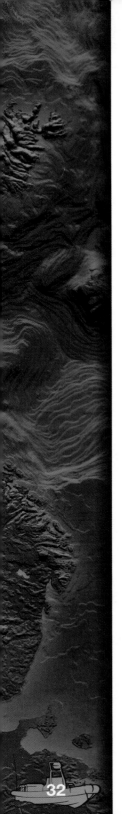